Thank GOD FOR...

Barbara Hollins

ISBN 979-8-89130-601-1 (paperback)
ISBN 979-8-89130-602-8 (digital)

Christian Faith Publishing
832 Park Avenue
Meadville, PA 16335
www.christianfaithpublishing.com

Printed in the United States of America

Acknowledgments

Thank God For is written to expose our youth to some accomplishments of the African American race. We are excited about the inventions and interventions to which the African American race has contributed.

This book does not encompass all the great and wonderful inventions and interventions by African Americans. It is designed to encourage parents, children, and teachers to delve deeper into the historical facts of the African American community.

Thank God for the idea and resources to write this book. Thank God for all the authors and the information available to research and formulate this book. Thank God for all those who helped me compile this book and those who prayed for it to reach many homes. My major encourager and technical supporter (computer), along with his editorial comments, is my husband, James R. Hollins Sr. He kept me going when I seemed to flounder. I thank my son, James R. Hollins Jr., for promoting the book on social media. My son, Dwayne A. Hollins, supported my illustrations by using his camera for pictures and their enhancements. Thanks to my son, Michael G. Hollins Sr., for editing the book and publishing details.

Thank God for adults reading this book to young children. This book may have words with which the children are not familiar, so I encourage the adults to explain these words, and the children will have words to add to their vocabulary.

Thank God for the United States Federal Patent.

A United States patent allows a person to invent or improve an idea and claim it as their own. It means that no one else can take their idea, sell it, or make it or use it without their permission for a time. Our book will use the word *patent* for each invention and intervention named to give credit to the inventor for their work.

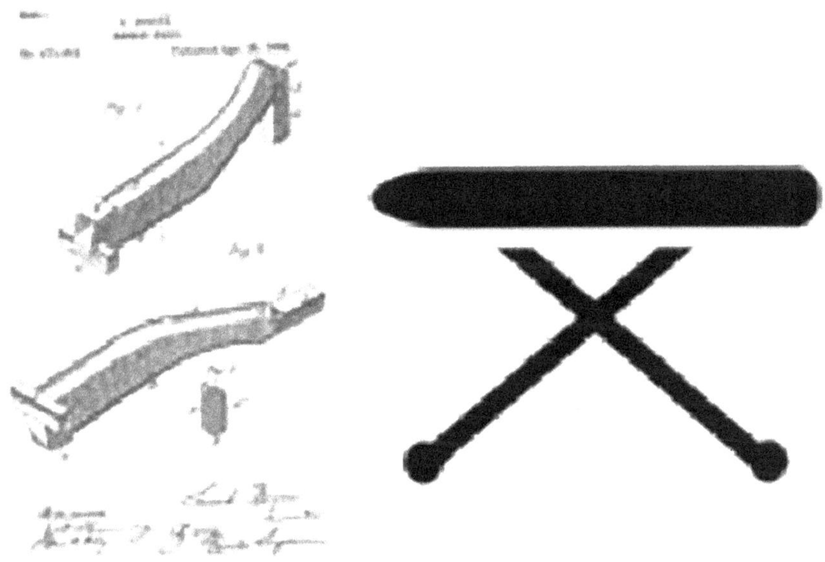

Thank God for ironing boards and for Sarah Boone, who received a patent for her invention of the ironing board. Now we have an easier way to take the wrinkles out of our clothes. We still use this type of board today.

Patent #473.563   April 26, 1892   SandeKennedy.com

Thank God for the shoe-lacing machines and Jan Matzlieger, who received a patent for his invention. The lasting machine sewed the top of the shoe to the bottom of the shoe. The machine produced shoes faster and easier and made shoes cost less.

Patent #423.937   March 25, 1890   www.Myblackhistory.net

Thank God for straightening combs made to make very curly hair straight and for Walter Sammons, who received a patent for his invention. This changed the way African Americans could wear their hair if they desired.

Patent #1,362,823   December 21, 1920   Microsoft Bing

Thank God for the automatic clothes dryer and George T. Sampson, who received a patent for his invention of the clothes dryer. This allowed people to dry their clothes faster and easier.

Patent #476.416   June 7, 1992   *George T. Sampson, SamePassage*

Thank God for the hairbrush and for Lyda Newman, who received a patent for a new and improved model of the hairbrush. It was a better design for African Americans' curly hair.

Patent #614.335   November 15, 1898   www.Bing.com/Images

Thank God for the wringing mop and Thomas Stewart, who made important improvements to the mop and received a patent. We can now squeeze our mop out without touching the mophead or removing the mop head for washing. This made it easier for the person to mop the floor.

Patent #499.402   June 11, 1893   Microsoft Bing and ThoughtCo.com

Thank God for hair-growing products and Madam C. J. Walker for her combination of mixtures to give African Americans' healthy hair. Her company received many patents for her products. People now have products that help them nourish their hair.

Patent #1,693515   November 27, 1928   African American Registry

Thank God for the portable pencil sharpener and John Love, who received a patent for his invention of the portable pencil sharpener. We don't need to use a knife to sharpen our pencils when the leads break or get dull anymore.

Patent #594.114   November 23, 1897   Pencils.com and USPTO

Thank God for the fountain pen and William Purvis, who received a patent for improving it. People can use these pens to write notes and letters to friends.

Patent #419.065   January 7, 1890   blackpast.org

Thank God for *paper bags and William Purvis* for his patented invention of an improved machine that made paper bags. It makes carrying groceries easier.

First patent #293353   Date: September
22, 1891   www.google patents

Another patent# 460,093A

Thank God for electric railway switches and William Purvis for this patented invention. Trains could move from a railroad track to another railroad track without stopping. This invention would prevent a lot of train wrecks.

Patent #419,065   Date August 17, 1897   Webuyblack.com

Thank God for the automatic gearshifts and Richard Spikes, who invented the gear and received a patent for the invention. It is the forerunner of the automatic gearshifts used today. Cars are easier to drive because of his insight into automobiles.

Patent #1,889.814   December 6, 1932   AARegistry.com

Thank God for the supercharge system and Joseph Gamell, its inventor, who received a patent. This invention allows our cars to have more power. This invention did not improve gas mileage.

Patent #3948.235   June 2, 1992   http//:patents.Justin.com

Thank God for the automatic traffic light and Garrett A. Morgan, who received a patent for his improvements. This invention made it safer for cars and trucks to take turns while moving through the streets. Many accidents are prevented because of the traffic light.

Patent #1,475,074   November 20, 1923   Automotivehistory.org.

Thank God for the gas mask and Garrett A. Morgan, who received a patent for this invention. This invention allowed people to go into unsafe rooms. Many lives are saved because of the gas mask.

Patent #1113675   October 13, 1914   USPTO and Thoughtco.com

Thank God for an improvement on the icebox (refrigerators). Thank God for John Stanard, who received a patent for improving the way we keep food cold. Electric refrigeration was not yet made.

Patent #455.891   July 14, 1891   Thoughtco.com

Thank God for an improvement on the oil stove. Thank God for John Stanard, who received a patent for improving the places where we could cook food. This stove was smaller and could be used in different places.

Patent #413,689   October 29, 1889   Thoughtco.com

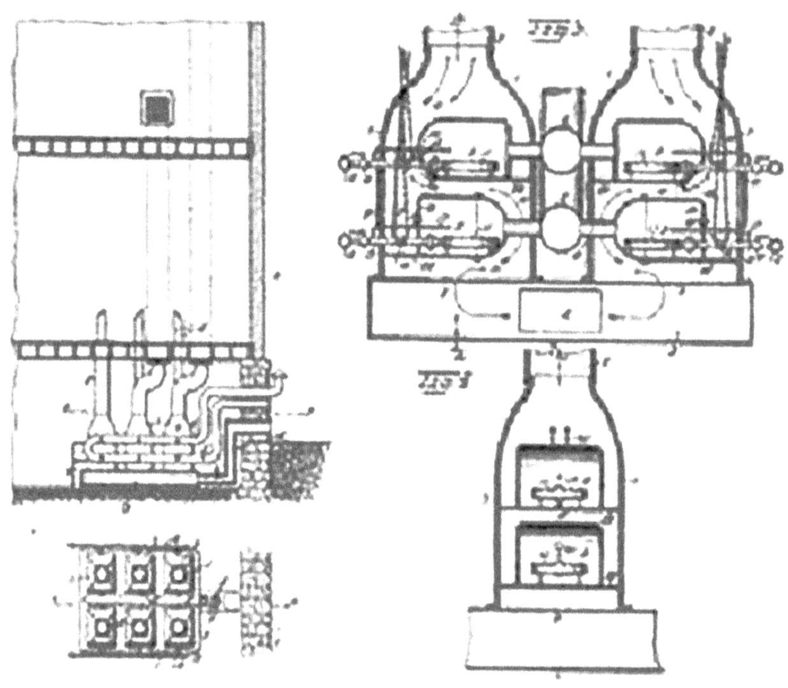

(Actual patent print)

Thank God for the gas furnaces and for Alice Parker, their inventor, who received a patent. This invention allowed the homeowners to heat the whole house with gas and eliminated the need to chop wood.

Patent #1,325,905   December 23, 1919   Energynews.network

Thank God for refrigerated trucks and Frederick Jones and his friend Numero. He received a patent for his invention, which allowed trucks to keep food cold or frozen for a long time. Then fruits and vegetables could be carried to other places and stay fresh.

Patent #2,475.841   July 12, 1949   ThoughtCo.com and NyongesaSande.com

Thank God for the automatic opening and closing of elevator doors and for Alexander Miles, who invented them and received a patent. These doors prevented people from falling down elevator shafts when the doors were left open.

Patent #371.207   October 11, 1887   Wikipedia.org

Thank God for mailboxes and Philip Downing, the inventor. He received a patent for this invention. Before this invention, people had to go to the post office to mail a letter. After this invention, they could go to corners where the mailboxes were placed to mail a letter.

Patent #462,096   October 27, 1891   Google Patents

Thank God for the light bulb filament (thread) that helped the bulb to last longer and for Lewis Howard Latimer, who received a patent for inventing the filament inside the bulb. Our light bulbs burn longer because of this invention.

Patent #252,386   September/1881   www.inv.org and Microsoft Bing

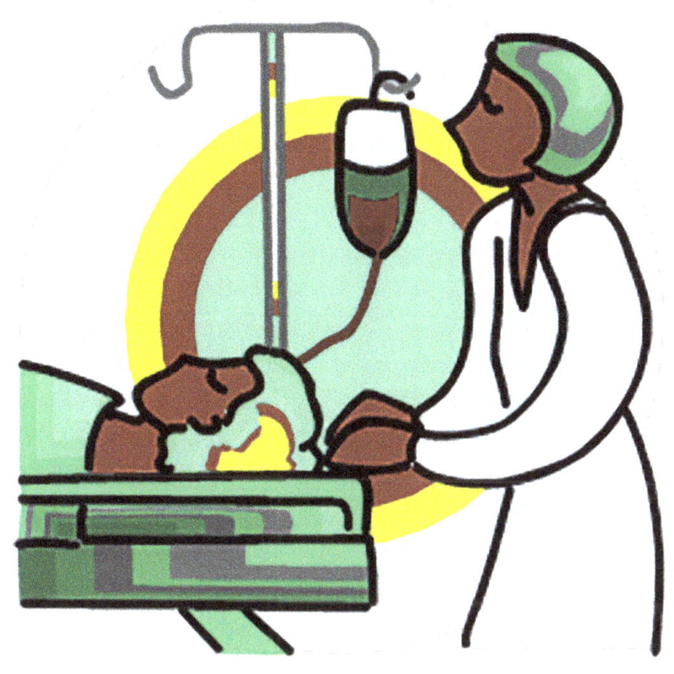

Thank God for the ability to receive blood (plasma) when needed (blood transfusion), and thank God for Charles Drew, who shared this knowledge of storing the blood until used. This process was patented.

Patent #2,389,355   November 10, 1942   www.invent.org   NyongeseSande.com

Thank God for the fun toy "Super Soaker" and Lonnie Johnson, who invented it and received a patent. His invention allowed children to have a great time with the super soaker.

Patent #5,074,437   December 24, 1991   Nyongesa Sande. com and Bing.com/images

Thank God for dry cleaners and Thomas Jennings, who received a patent, for combining the right chemicals to clean clothes without water. Many clothes are now dry-cleaned because of his chemical combinations.

Patent #US 3,306X   March 3, 1821   www.thoughtco.com/ThomasJennings

Thank God for the peanut and other crops and for George Washington Carver, who produced over three hundred items from the peanut. He did not create peanut butter, but he made flour, soap, shaving cream, antiseptic paints, stains, and many, many more usable products. By choice, he only patented three of his products.

Patent #1,632365   June 14, 1927   Suiter/
Swantz Intellectual Property

References

Henry, Carma. "What If There Were No Black Folks." Westside Gazette.com.

Patents. https://www.findlaw.com.

Boone, Sarah. 1832–1904. biography.com. Blackpast.org.

Boone, Sarah. Invention, ironing board, and facts. Biography.com.

Matzeliger, Jan. Biography.com. http://postal museum.si.edu/exhibition/the black-experience-business leaders-and inventors/janmatzeliger.

Sammons, Walter. https://theinventors.org/library/inventors/bl_Walter_Sammons.htm.

https://urbanareas.net/info/sammons-walter-inventor.

Sampson, George T., https://www.bing.com/.

Sampson, George T. SamePassage.

Sampson, George T. Developer of America's First. https://www.appliancesconnection.com/blog/americas.

Newman, Lyda. Biography, life, interesting facts. https://wwwthoughtco.com/inventor-lyda-newman

www.sunsigns.org/famousbirthdays/profile/lyda-newman/.

Bellis, Mary. "Thomas W. Stewart, Inventor of the Wringing Mop." ThoughtCo. July 31, 2021. http://www.thoughtco.com/thomas-stewart-the-mop-4077038.

Bellis, Mary. "Biography of Madam C.J. Walker, American Entrepreneur and Beauty Mogul."

ThoughtCo. September 9, 2021, thoughtco.com/madame-c-j-walker-1992677.

Bellis, Mary. "John Lee Love, Portable Pencil Sharpener Inventor." ThoughtCo. August 28, 2020. thoughtco.com/john-lee-love-profile-1992097.

Walker, C. J.www.pbs.org/wnet/african-americans-many-rivers-to-cross/history/.

Wikipedia. William B. Purvis. *en.wikipedia.org/wiki/William_B._Purvis.*

https:www.blackpast.org/African-american-history/purvis-william.

www.google patents.

Webuyblack.com.

"Frederick Jones, The Inventors." www:thoughtco.com/Frederick-mckinley-jones.

Gammel, Joseph A. https://patents.justia.com/inventor/joseph-a-gammel

Richard Spikes, Mahoney, E. (November 11, 2017). Richard Spikes (1878–1965) BlackPast.org. https//wwwblackpast.org/african-american-history/spikes-richard-1878-1965/.

https://theblackdetour.com/Richard-spikes-invented.

Bellis, Mary. "Biography of Garrett Morgan, Inventor of the Gas Mask." ThoughtCo. August 29, 2020. Thoughtco.com/garrett-morgan-profile-1992160.

Garland, Kassidy. "Garrett Morgan and the Invention of the Traffic Light." https:www.funtimesmagazine.com/2020/11/20/335100.

Bellis, Mary. "Biography of John Stanard, Inventor of a Better.

Refrigerator." www.ThoughtCo. February 16, 2021. thoughtco.com/john-standard-inventor-1991315.

Parker, Alice. November 11, 2017. www.geni.com/people/Inventor-of-the-heating-furnace-Alice-PARKER/60000000E.

Alexander Miles | Lemelson. https://lemelson.mit.edu/resources/alexander-miles.

Wikipedia.org.

"Phillip Downing." https://www.blackpast.org/african-american-history/downing-philip-b.

Lewis Howard Latimer. www.invent.org and Microsoft Bing.

Charles Drew. www.invent.org.

Lonnie Johnson. bing.com/images.

Thomas Jennings. www.thought.com/ThomasJennings.

George Washington Carver. Suiter/Swantz Intellectual Property.

Clipart from Print Artist Program.

About the Author

Barbara J. Hollins is a first-time publisher of a book. As a child, she wrote various children's stories without any intent to publish them. She also wrote a children's church manual as suggestions for teachers of children for her own use. She compiled a manual for parents, with the permission of various authors, as a resource booklet.

Black history is the passion of this author. As a child, she was denied information about the accomplishments of this great and intelligent group, and the schools did not teach a lot about black history and accomplishments. There was a lot of information available about the great works of our forefathers, but it was not taught in our schools. She is thanking God for all the information on the Internet and in published books available to educate herself and others.

Barbara Hollins was born in Mobile, Alabama, and graduated from Williamson High School. She lives in Flint, Michigan, with her husband, James. She holds a BA degree in sociology from Stillman College in Tuscaloosa, Alabama, and a master of social work degree from the University of Michigan in Ann Arbor, Michigan.